The Leper's Fire and Other Poems

Mapfumo Clement Chihota

First published in Great Britain in 2024 by:

Carnelian Heart Publishing Ltd
Suite A
82 James Carter Road
Mildenhall
Suffolk
IP28 7DE
UK
www.carnelianheartpublishing.co.uk

©Mapfumo Clement Chihota 2024

Paperback ISBN   978-1-914287-63-3
eBook ISBN   978-1-914287-64-0

All rights reserved. No part of this publication may be reproduced, stored in a retrieval system or transmitted in any form or by any means, electronic, mechanical, photocopying, recording or otherwise without prior written permission from the publisher.

Editors: Marian Christie and
Samantha Rumbidzai Vazhure

Cover design:
Artwork – Chitende Fine Art
Layout - Rebeca Covers

Interior:
Typeset by Carnelian Heart Publishing Ltd
Layout and formatting by DanTs Media

CONTENTS

A. THE POEMS WHICH I WRITE

The poems which I write	10
Morning inspiration	11
Dead on arrival	12
Futile fights	13

B. THOSE ABOVE AND THOSE BELOW

Those above and those below	15
When you turn thirty	18
Respecting the mascot	19
The leper's fire	20
The rich and the poor	21
Crying boy	22
Answer of the ancestors	23
Nehanda	27

C. SONGFUL DREAM

Dance gently to the drum	29
Stolen pleasures	30
Songful dream	31
Othello	32
No!	33
Stormy tears	34
Two-forked tongues	35
Did I come here to cook sadza?	36
Princely boasting	38
Pam	39

D. EARTH, POOR EARTH

Beetles	41
Mosquito	42
Earth, poor earth	43

	Sweet amnesia	44
	Did you notice?	45
	Oh, no God, not again!	46
E.	**IF**	
	If	49
	Thanks	50
	Illusions	51
	Diversion	52
	Euphemisms	53
	Coolness	54
	Luck	55
	Killing time	56
	The hard one	57
	Choice	58
	The visit of the Lord	59
	The white man I met	60

To the memory of my dear father, Clement Chihota Senior,
who eloquently expressed himself with saxophone, guitar and voice.

A. THE POEMS WHICH I WRITE

THE POEMS WHICH I WRITE

The poems which I write
are squeezed out of my mind
each time I'm in a plight....

Sometimes,
they drip out on their own
like drops of honey from a hive
when the bees are sleeping.

MORNING INSPIRATION

Like an innocuous snake
visiting to remove rodents from the garden,
the pen was discovered
amongst a sheaf of yellowing papers.

Its lined body felt cool, and supple.
Its wet mouth began to drool
tender lines
of early morning poetry.

DEAD ON ARRIVAL

Sometimes poems stumble into my head
mumble, fumble then tumble-down dead!

Such poems say nothing
Mean nothing
Or hide something?

I bury
Their crumpled cadavers
without ceremony
Or palaver.

FUTILE FIGHTS

There is no doubt
no doubt at all, that louts
bout in bloody brawls
then shout victory like scouts
discovering spouts
of poisoned water.

B. THOSE ABOVE AND THOSE BELOW

THOSE ABOVE AND THOSE BELOW

I

A soft foot
in a hard leather shoe
knocks against a hard foot
in a soft plastic sandal
and there is pain.

Rain
pelts peddlers pushing peanuts on the pavement
in penthouses high above
others hardly know it is raining.

II

A lame pedestrian
hobbling past a cheap and chuntering bar
was smashed against the tar…

The car…
was driven by the Olympic gold medallist
in sprinting.

When rain
repeated its trick on splashing peddlers
laughter
from underground cellars
decked with tortoiseshell and ormolu
gurgled to the surface.

> Cellists and fiddlers
> adjusted the timbre of their instruments
> to blend
> with the distant hailstone crackle.
> And the degustation continued….

III

When valleys fill with water
mountains laugh
and as pits are dug deeper
soil dumps grow.

The snail
crossing a stretch of sand
blistered by the sun
and floundering
like an antediluvian dhow
caught in the doldrums
is watched
in amusement, by birds
preening themselves in mopane trees
high above the tragedy.

The birds
        dream
                of sun-soaked excursions
                        to faraway places.

IV

Feathers rustling
like newly minted bills
the bird bristled into a café
then stopped short, undecided:
       Would it be a pie, a pizza or a pancake?

Shell rattling like loose copper coins
the snail sidled into the café
then stopped short, wondering
       Whether to grab a bun, swallow, then go to jail
            or fail, faint and go to hell?

V

All this was before Noah's flood returned
to sweep away the debris of pride and prejudice
and fill up yawning pits
with the heads
of mountains.

WHEN YOU TURN THIRTY

When you turn thirty
with no prospects and a future all murky,
do you curl up and wish yourself unborn?
Or do you feel the first stirrings of anger?

When all colleges say they are full
the police and army say, "You are too old.
Where were you all these years?"
The industries retrench those already there,
and farmers frown suspiciously at labourers seeking
work in English,

do you accept your lot with grace
and say, "So goes life," like a good citizen?

Or do red spots begin to dance before your eyes
and, like the taunted bull,
charge the nimble, dancing matador
and the red flag that he waves

to trample both to dust
then sniff and look around
for the clowns who organised this show
in the first place?

RESPECTING THE MASCOT

Black goat
mincing in red and gold coat
stay close to your handler!

The cheering crowd
clapping and jeering loud
longs for hot goat meat.

Their tattered clothes
flapping and fluttering like moths
could easily be replaced
by that red and gold treasure
That you wear.

THE LEPER'S FIRE

Have you seen the leper's fire
flickering upon the mountainside
like an angry eye
on a cold winter night?

Fingerless palm pushes green log into
fuming fire
wet wood weeps waxy tears of
frustration
tall twig poker pokes deep
into belly of fire
        that aborts red sparks
        that turn to cold ash
        on grey skin.

Are you waiting for dawn by this flickering mountainside fire–
or sliding back to the whitened valleys below
where skeletons of alien fire-makers
glow with a nostalgic phosphorescence?

Or, like a beggarly turncoat
pushing on to the mountain-top above
bright with electrical light
where extortionate angels smirk upon your arrival
then ask how much gold or *ngoda*

you managed to smuggle
on your way up?

THE RICH AND THE POOR

When the rusty prison gates of Marxism
creaked open, at last
we rushed out, singing praise songs
to our liberators....

Who ushered us
into a giant auditorium
where sweating butchers, meat-cleavers in hand
cut and pruned off
burdensome humanity.

The massacre began.
Bodies were trenched and retrenched
in polished mass graves
prepared by economic engineers....

As the massacre intensified
blood rose
to window level.

Powerful politicians
fashioned rafts out of tables and trestles.

The weak
were thrown overboard
to drown, chained and weighed down
by carapaces of their own poverty.

Round two of the war had begun
the rich and the poor were at each other's throats again,
openly this time
And without
Any 'isms' to disguise the vendetta.

CRYING BOY

Tapfuma must go and sell eggs
early in the morning
while other children go to school.

Tapfuma's father died in the war
before Tapfuma was born.

Tapfuma walks barefoot
his wet feet slapping against the tarmac.

Tapfuma has one green jersey
which is fraying at the hems
and one pair of khaki shorts
that has endured many winters.

Today
Tapfuma is crying
not because it's so cold
or because he is not in school,
but because his mother slapped him
when she didn't really want to slap him.

The man who came home with mother last night
was drunk, giggling, and angry
and carried an okapi knife.

He made mother laugh
in a loud shrill voice.

In the middle of the night
he got up, going to the loo
then tripped against Tapfuma
who slept near the door.

He kicked and swore
and called Tapfuma a fool
then asked mother
why she kept such a big boy
in her room.

Early in the morning
there was a sharp argument on the bed
and mother told Tapfuma
to get up and leave.

Tapfuma pointed out that it was
too early.
Few people buy boiled eggs,
at five o'clock in the morning.

The man on the bed laughed harshly
as mother got up,
pulled the blanket from Tapfuma
then slapped him three times
on the cheeks.

But Tapfuma could tell
she did not really want to beat him
and was sad and sorry that she had to.

Tapfuma became sad and sorry for his mother
That is why he is crying....

ANSWER OF THE ANCESTORS

The dollar fell into a pit.
We thought it had reached the bottom,
then it fell into a pit inside the pit.

Citizens
scattered to seek sachets of saccharin binned in foreign lands.
And denizens, left behind,
tried to dredge a living from the sour peat surrounding the lips of the pit.

Miners among daughters and sons of the land
volunteered to go down first.
They were heard, digging
between the ribs and spine of the land.
They were heard grunting
And tugging....

Then came out complaining
there were rocks down there which jackhammers could not bore,
and seams which stubbornly refused to give up their ore.

Thus began the lore
that our dollar had fallen into a pit of a pit of a pit.

Panners demanded to try their luck next.
They were seen
using sieves and dishes
to deceive gold grains out of riverbeds and beaver dams.
The ancestors frowned....

Farmers of the land formed a union
layered and potent like an onion.
A brilliant idea was peeled out:
How about growing a tall strain of tobacco?
Able to reach the surface from the bottom of the pit?

Magicians with knowledge of plants (including mandrakes – and why
Reuben was so excited to find them growing in his field) provided the
tobacco seedling,
which grew and multiplied swiftly.

The farmers jubilated.
They sibilated in excitement as they shinned down stems
and ululated
when they discovered secrets hidden underground.

"Down there in the pit
are tunnels that can channel
hard-earned money to foreign bank accounts.
The tunnel is even equipped with runnels!"
they whispered to each other
as they climbed out.

Peasants
libating on the screes of rocky dwalas
pleaded to be sent down too with their hoes and mattocks.
Everyone roared with laughter.
"Silly ignoramuses – are they thinking with their buttocks?"
The ancestors winced.

The industrialists of the land
proposed a powerful synergy
sizzling with zeal and energy.

Roping themselves together
They rappelled one by one into the pit.
They were seen gesturing
as they disappeared from view.
They were heard speculating
as they went even deeper.

They later came out admitting
they had actually extended the depth of the pit.
Their rope had snapped
and to save themselves
they had to build niches and footholds
using greenback rocks, of sterling quality,
mined from the bottom of the pit....

At this point
The ancestors shuddered
And earth itself juddered

and sundered
sinking the dollar
into a pit underneath the pit of the pit of the pit.

NEHANDA

Broad feet planted like buttressed
banyan beams,
you stared past the glass-eyed box
recording a detail of the present.

Past the pot-bellied white boy
smoking and smirking
in his shining leather boots.

Past the towering black-watchers
ambiguous in thick white puttees
wrapped over bare cracked feet.

Past guns and machine guns
bristling all around.
Past a wordy death sentence
lisped by tobacco-stained lips in a foreign language.
Past the thick strong noose
imported from Britain....

Past even now
to a future
pregnant
with promise
and vindication.

C.   SONGFUL DREAM

DANCE GENTLY TO THE DRUM

Dance gently to the drum, my love
for the night is going to be long.

Be slow, like the leopard.
Do not eat while running, like the hyena.

One large person cannot surround a mound.
Finger and thumb are both needed to crush a bug.

Twinned
like two nuts within their shell
we will snuggle
through the struggle
of this thunderous night

till daylight cracks our pod.

STOLEN PLEASURES

Soft stolen pleasures
backfire like pneumatic chisels
cracking a well-trodden path
to expose rotten piping.

Supplementary sex by the seaside
converts
to charred memories
which break
and scatter
like cinder.

Sudorific efforts
Sudsing brief orbs of sweetness
dessicate
into the rough granular buff
of the clerk of court's envelope
demanding child support.

SONGFUL DREAM

Babet,
Sing again, that motet
of love and lingerie.
Sing again that duet
the one first heard at that motel
where Morbeous died a petroleum death.

Georgette,
You, the one from Niger,
lionise the song,
lintel it with your contralto
and moor the dream
that we all share.

So we all lived this songful dream
which swam inside our consciousness until we were awoken by a scream:
Babet, singer of the motet
weeping for Morbeous.

OTHELLO

Murderous thoughts
mooching about inside the mind
of a Moor:

Did she
did she not?

Massaged statistics
whispered evidence
bitter-sweet
like mordant humour
in euphonious verse.

Did she not
did she?

Can anyone know?

NO!

Shall I sever this affair
which grows out of me
like a mole
and graft a new one
onto its place?

STORMY TEARS

"I've found you a place to train
at Nyadire Teachers' College,"
the elated husband announced
to his baby-suckling wife.

She froze.
Cold-tongued fear
licked her trembling insides.

Questions
strong as male baboons
gripped her
and raped her peace of mind.

What if...
and then how...
and why...?

Instead of voicing these questions
she burst into stormy tears
that he interpreted as the misery
of a woman
leaving her warm home
to go out into the cold
for a temporary while.

TWO-FORKED TONGUES

He got married to this woman
whose face appears ugly
but whose behind
rocks like two soft babies
dancing inside a blanket
when she walks.

Really?

Yes!
And she's only ugly
before she smiles.

What happens when she smiles?

Oh!
Her peppermint-white teeth
which look fresh enough to eat
have a little gap, slightly to one side....
Her dark eyes sparkle
like sun-pierced jewels
And then
she also has dimples.

Yaah?

Yes!

And what is her name?
Has she been to school?

She did a B.BS, B.Comm or something
Her name is Pamhi, Pemhi or something.
Anyway
she's very pregnant.

Oh really?
What a pity!

First published in The Herald newspaper (Zimbabwe), 2002

DID I COME HERE TO COOK SADZA?

My husband
you have become a weevil
working mischief
and evil.

You bore through leaves and sheaves of paper
as if they were some type of wafer
with an addictive flavour.

Your diet
of letters in the morning
words in the afternoon
and sentences in the evening
has given you a hard thick skin.

My cries
are now like echoes
which return to their source
without an answer.

The black ink
that

you drink
has changed your tongue from pink.

You now lie
that you will become a doctor
by reading poems.

You now lie
without winking
or thinking.

Do you think I came here to cook sadza
or that I came here to eat?
As if there was not enough sadza
in my own father's house?

Do you think I came here to play golf
since I now sleep alone
hands clasped tightly between my knees?

You need to come out of the bushel
and face the world.

Or else
buy me one tall, strong book
of my own.

PRINCELY BOASTING

Princess of Mutoko
standing tall as a gazelle
staring at me with black glowing eyes
that match that patch of sky
lit by the Milky Way
let me introduce myself.

I am Chihota, prince among the
Zvimbakupa
from Marondera.

My demesnes
sparsely treed and richly grassed
are flat and level like a stadium of fun.

White-pebbled rivers
rich in jade
crisscross the kingdom.

And honey
both treed and underground
flows almost as much as does the milk
from our heavy-uddered cows
whose teats trail in the grass.

In our land
we venerate the zebra
the most decorated of all animals.
Thus, we, the men of the Zvimbakupa clan,
are the black and white beads
which every proud woman
should put around her waist.

PAM

Sibling of my soul
in the rainy world of adolescence
you walked in the drizzle
shaking droplets of rain out of your hair
which hit me on the heart
soaking me in a film of innocence.

Your laughter
was Antarctic ice
breaking against the glass
of a restrictive aquarium.

Your eyes were pearls
formed within the wet womb
of an oyster.

Salt from the spray of distant seas
clung to your lips:

Those lips
of liquorice
and sherbet.

D. EARTH, POOR EARTH

BEETLES

They come flying in swarms
and strike against the lighted pane
like living hail falling slantwise
from a breaking sky.

They hum and cry in painful agitation,
"Light, light!
Towards light, we come!"

The few that have gained entry into the room
fly ecstatically around the naked bulb:
"At light! At light! We have
arrived at light!"

Reluctantly
I switch off the light, and,
as I get into bed,
I hear them thumping one by one
onto the cold hard floor

To crawl aimlessly in the dark
all night.

MOSQUITO

I sprayed my room with acrid aerosols
and choked on smoke from pungent coils
just to fix you.

I swatted my eye with a painful blow
and shrouded myself in a stifling net
just to spurn you.

And you waited
patiently
and hid yourself
carefully
just to bite me.

EARTH, POOR EARTH

Earth
poor earth
panting and gasping for rain

and yet tied to the ground
and unable
to yank down the sky
and ask the question,
why?

SWEET AMNESIA

Squatting
on cold dewy grass
soft as a baby's hair

and shielded
on one side
by lush green sisals
and on the other
by zinnias and marigolds,

He lost
his awareness
of time and location,
of status and position.

He forgot
his bank balances and bank overdrafts,
the boss who had fired him,
the mortgage in Harare
the plans and prospects.

He forgot
what the birds, lizards and bees
forgot
a long, long time ago.

Later,
he told himself
that the place must have been enchanted....

He should perhaps return
and clear up the mess.

DID YOU NOTICE?

That bad company
destroys the fresh appeal
of greenery
and scenery.

OH, NO GOD, NOT AGAIN!

"Old Nhengure has given birth
to two lovely eggs!"
Was the excited chatter
of the busybody little sparrow.

"Good news!" hooted the kind
wise owl.
"Let's go and see her,"
was the prompt decision
of Hohodza, the wood-pecker.

Old Nhengure herself
shying away in modesty
accepted their congratulations
but with a fearful heart.

Was this not the tenth time
they had come
with the same good wishes over
the same event?
And yet the precious little eggs
had always ended up
in the stomachs
of cats, little lemurs, or snakes.

With the approach of Autumn
Nhengure sat patiently over her eggs
and grew thin and haggard
as she never left the nest.

On the first day of Autumn,
It happened!
The warm shells cracked
and out wriggled two fluffy chicks.

Old Nhengure burst her heart with joy,
and crooned a strange song which rasped
out of her throat.

Soon she was combing through
the river banks
looking for worms and beetles
to stuff into the ever-open mouths
of her eager fledglings.

This was her life and joy
until the day
she came back
to find the nest
empty – again.

E. IF

IF

If Satan completely ruled this world
then no Satan-worshipper would be
able to cry, "Lucifer!"
before his throat was cut.

THANKS

The word dropped out of his mouth
like a foreign dime
loosed from the pockets of a man
hurrying for time.

ILLUSIONS

The illusions
of the beautiful
choke and irritate
like dust
raised for no reason
and slow to settle.

A DIVERSION

Tired thoughts
flutter this way and that
like butterflies
sick with the monotonous perfume
of a flowering scrubland

Will this end?

The question meanders
between barchans and seifs
of flowing protocol.

The chairperson drones on, and on,
his raspy voice sibilating at the edges.

This ends now!
A declaration
from a quick querulous fart
that stops the meeting
with rumbles
of laughter.

EUPHEMISMS

When Cicourel the cockerel was
killed
they dressed him
by plucking off his feathers
and stuffing his head, legs
and gizzard
into his belly.

The same thing happened
to the criminal who was executed
to the elephants which were culled
to the baby who was miscarried
to the enemy who was eliminated
to the poor under neoliberalism....

COOLNESS

She was cool but she burnt
underneath
like the soil at dusk
after a sweltering day.

LUCK

Like whisky doled out at a prisoners'
function
it comes in rare, single shots
and always runs out
too soon.

KILLING TIME

He ran his eyes along the length of
the bar:
all customers were well-watered
and conversations were flowing.

Then he settled back on his stool
closed his eyes and began to
hum a tune
tapping with one toe.

Killing time–
which was slowly killing him.

THE HARD ONE

She smiled heavily and when she
laughed
it was like a mother duck cackling
sadly
to her brood of chicks.

Sadness rang there
but indistinct, like a bell muffled in thick cloth.

I imagined tears falling
and wetting the dry crow's feet around
her arid eyes,
I wished she would simply cry
and her tears gush out like springs
from a desert rock
springs shooting but boulder-piercing arrows.

Instead
my own tears
contained in large milk bottles
somewhere behind my eyes
spilt out of a crack
making her sneer
and then laugh again.

CHOICE

Blind
but continuously moving
like the restless maggot
I fumbled forward
changing directions.

Through stagnant pools
and mounds of dirt
and slimes of gob
I ventured

Searching for the place called
"Yearn no more."

At some point
I burst into a fly
that can now distinguish between
milk and filth
and fly to either place
out of choice.

THE VISIT OF THE LORD

When the Lord came down to visit
the earth
snippets and gobbets of news
overwhelmed him.

His faithful
were eating and drinking
and lusting.
His faithful
were meddling
with money.

The faithless
worshipped the brains within their skulls
which they trained to be scientific
and rational
and objective.
The faithless
calculated mathematically
the probability of end-time.

But despite their rationality
they ate
and drank
and sucked
and slumbered.

THE WHITE MAN I MET

He did not flinch
when I walked close to his car.
He did not panic
when I brushed against his pocket.
He did not smile to himself or patronise
when he heard me talking.

He did not frown or smirk or
quirk his mouth
as he listened to me.
He did not get startled
when I made an intelligent remark.
He did not think it was a special concession
to listen as I talked.

He did not giggle
when we discussed African politics
nor wiggle a finger
at African presidents.
He did not believe
that all Africans were inherently corrupt
or begrudge Africans
for having all this melanin.

He did not contradict himself
by worshipping Tina Turner and
Michael Jackson
while abhorring the sight
of the mujibhas and chimbwidos
in his immediate environment.

That white man
was probably Jesus.

www.ingramcontent.com/pod-product-compliance
Lightning Source LLC
Chambersburg PA
CBHW012100090526
44591CB00019B/2718